FATHERS AND SONS

Michael Bradford

BROADWAY PLAY PUBLISHING INC
New York
www.broadwayplaypublishing.com
info@broadwayplaypublishing.com

Cover art by Mark Gerard McKee

First edition: May 2017
I S B N: 978-0-88145-420-8

Book design: Marie Donovan
Page make-up: Adobe InDesign
Typeface: Palatino
Printed and bound in the U S A

FATHERS AND SONS had the following readings and productions: Lark Play Development Center (NYC): Developed and Staged Reading (2009); Hygienic Art Park (New London, Connecticut): Staged Reading (2010); A C T (Seattle, Washington): Premiere Production (2010); eta Creative Arts (Chicago, Illinois): Production (2012); Negro Ensemble Company at the Signature Theatre at Pershing Square; Reading (2014).

The cast and creative contributors of the Premiere at A C T were as follows:

LEON GOODWATER.....................................William Hall Jr
MARCUS GOODWATER ....Reginald Andre Jackson
YVETTE GOODWATER ....Tracey A Leigh
BENARD GOODWATER.....................................Wilber Penn

Director... Valerie Curtis-Newton
Scenic designer.. Matthew Smucker
Costume designer..........................Melanie Taylor Burgess
Lighting designer ....L B Morse
Sound designer...Eric Chappelle
Stage manager... Jeffrey K Hanson
Assistant stage manager ....Nora Menkin

CHARACTERS & SETTING

MARCUS GOODWATER, *age is late 20s, early 30s / Navy veteran and Iraq war veteran, husband to* YVETTE */ father of Stephen / son of* LEON */ grandson of* BENARD

YVETTE GOODWATER, *age is late 20s, early 30s / wife of* MARCUS */ mother of Stephen*

LEON GOODWATER, *age is late 40s-50s / father of* MARCUS */ son of* BENARD

BENARD GOODWATER, *age is "Dead", this actor can be older or younger than* LEON *and still reasonably support the generational aesthetic.*

The set is the foyer and living room of an apartment on an upper floor of a building along Riverside Drive, Harlem, NY. The rest of the apartment is off stage. The Apartment has a huge "picture window" which looks out over the Hudson River. The structure and language of the play allow for the "window" not to exist in reality, but in the imagination of the audience.

ACT ONE

(BENARD *enters the dark apartment wiping down his horn, singing, "Salt peanuts, salt peanuts." He is old and dead, dressed in a gray "shark skin" suit, straight legs, Stacey Adams two-tone shoes and Pork-pie hat. Fifties Jazz club style. He sits on a chair or perhaps on the arm of the couch. He clears and tests his horn. Lights dimly rise.)*

BENARD: Folk wanna tell you living is hard. Really, ain't nothing too hard about it. Harold might tell you there ain't nothing hard as war, no better test of a man's resolve. But I'm here to tell you, a man is just as subject to be a casualty of a woman, as he is a casualty of war. Now in a war you ain't required to die but one time. But a woman? Please, you cain't *count* the number of times you liable to give up the ghost. If you ain't been here but a minute! you know what I'm talking 'bout. You cain't even get a breath in the space between a war and the kind of hell a woman can put you through.

But that's just part of life. You see, the trick is not to forget, self preservation is the first law of nature and only a fool would even wanna *try* and buck nature. You understand that, and "hard" is a relative thing. Make sure when the dust clears, you the one standing. Hell, that's just common mother wit sense. Everything else…is salt peanuts. Don't take my word on it. Just ask Diz. "Salt peanuts, salt peanuts…"

(BENARD *plays a few bars as* MARCUS *enters the living room from the outside door and turns on the lights to right now, this minute, in his apartment, 8th floor, Riverside Drive, Harlem, New York. The apartment is well furnished and nicely laid out. A huge picture window downstage looks out over the city. He's been out all day. He takes off his backpack, takes a worm map out of the backpack and spreads it out, then takes a gun out the backpack and puts it on top of the map. He takes a marker and starts to "check" different locations on the map. The house phone rings, but it is not a "real" sound, it is more like a dream, an echo. He watches the phone for a minute then tries it anyway. It continues echoing even as he speaks.)*

MARCUS: Hello? Hello! ...Detective? ...Vette?

(*He hangs up the phone and the echoing stops. The door intercom buzzes. He walks to the huge picture window that looks out over the city. The intercom buzzes again. He answers it.)*

MARCUS: Yes? Yes? Press the button that says "answer".

(*Over the speaker.)*

LEON: It's...Leon. It's your father.

(MARCUS *hits the buzzer to let Leon in.)*

MARCUS: Damn. I don't believe you really came.

(MARCUS *picks up the gun and puts it in a nearby drawer. He takes a leather pouch out of the same drawer and puts it in his pocket. He stares at the backpack for a moment. The lights shift to "memory" and* YVETTE *enters from the kitchen, a bit breathless.* BENARD *moves down to the window.)*

YVETTE: There you are! You later than I thought you'd be. (*She looks back down the hallway.)* Stephen! Wash your hands, baby—

MARCUS: Yvette.

YVETTE: Well I hope you fed your poor son something other than ice cream all day— *(She eyes his for a minute, teasing.)* —well I guess not. Let me warm up dinner— *(She starts to enter the kitchen.)* —and please make sure he actually *washes* his hands—

MARCUS: Yvette.

YVETTE: Something wrong? You ate some mess on the street, didn't you? What did you feed my poor child? Stephen! Baby, mommy is—!

(YVETTE exits down the hallway and returns after a moment. MARCUS shakes his head "no" through the rest of this.)

YVETTE: You left him with my sister…with Nina…the Alston's, he's playing with Dante—

MARCUS: Yvette—

YVETTE: Stop saying my name and tell me what is going on. Where is Stephen?

(The trumpet kicks in.)

YVETTE: Alright Marcus, you're scaring me.

MARCUS: Vette—

YVETTE: Ok. Right now. Just go and get my baby.

MARCUS: I can't.

YVETTE: 'cuse me?

(MARCUS moves to YVETTE, she backs away.)

YVETTE: Yes you can, you can go and get him because he's your son you can—

MARCUS: I can't.

YVETTE: What do you mean you- he left here with you, Marcus, just this morning, with you, with his daddy, with *that* backpack. *(She starts across the room then returns.)*

Alright. Alright. Then you need to take me to wherever he…you can tell me on the way what hap— …let me get my… Where is Stephen?!

(Silence)

MARCUS: I don't know.

YVETTE: You don't know?

(Lights full up as Yvette slowly backs off down the "hallway". Marcus returns to "now." The sounds of the street waft in. After a moment there is a knock at the door and Marcus answers it. His father, Leon, stands in the doorway, a suitcase in hand, his clothes outdated and worn. He is an older version of the young man. They shake hands. Leon notices Benard immediately. Benard's horn sounds off.)

LEON: Boy, you still got that grip.

MARCUS: Yeah.

(LEON steps into the apartment.)

LEON: Good to see you. *(Silence)* I know this a bit'a surprise.

MARCUS: Granny called this morning, told me you were coming.

LEON: *(Laughing)* That's good.

MARCUS: Why didn't you call?

LEON: Wanted to. Didn't know what to say. Tried to come soon as your Granny told me about your boy, but it took me a minute to come up with the airfare. Hell, I still be sitting at the airport if you ain't helped me with the car fare. *(Silence)* Cain't remember the last time I flew. They checks everything now, don't they. Made me take off my shoes and—

MARCUS: They make everybody—

LEON: They don't make everybody.

MARCUS: Right.

LEON: Went through my clothes, my bags, like I'm some kind of—

MARCUS: I got it. Here. *(Silence)* The thing you couldn't pack. 'Cause of the way they checks the bags these days. I got it. Here.

(MARCUS pulls the leather pouch out of his pocket. BENARD and the trumpet sound off, a shrill blast, a quick run.)

LEON: That's not what I was talking 'bout.

MARCUS: I'm just saying—

LEON: If I'm talking about somebody going through my bags, I'm talking 'bout somebody going through my bags.

MARCUS: Right.

LEON: Let me make sure I got this straight. Your grandmother called just this morning?

MARCUS: Yeah.

LEON: And in the space 'tween then and now, with everything you got going on, you found the time to take yourself out into the street—

MARCUS: I'm already in the street all day / everyday

LEON: and bought some—

MARCUS: Yeah. I bought some.

LEON: I see. All right. You just walked out the front door and into the street 'cause you know where to go and—

MARCUS: It's nice right here but you go two blocks, anything you need.

LEON: Ain't like it used to be. With that. Nothing like it used to be.

MARCUS: Really?

LEON: I look like I need that?

BENARD: Yep.

MARCUS: I don't live that kind of life, so I wouldn't know what "that" looks like.

LEON: Ain't here but a couple days. This how it's gone be?

(MARCUS *puts the pouch back in the drawer it came from.* LEON *points to the drawer the leather pouch was put into.*)

LEON: You listen to second hand talk, you put yourself in a bad position.

MARCUS: Right.

LEON: You got enough on your plate.

MARCUS: I know what I got on my plate.

LEON: I asked you for car fare. I ain't ask you for…that.

(*Silence.* MARCUS *picks up* LEON's *suitcase and exits up the hallway. The trumpet sounds off again. To* BENARD.)

LEON: What in the hell you doing here?

BENARD: Just about to ask you the same damn thing. A week ago you was slobbering like a baby, pissin' yourself.

LEON: I ain't thinking 'bout you.

BENARD: Don't matter none to me where I am. Long as Mugg know where to find me.

LEON: Anybody looking for you know just where to find you, Benard Goodwater, under six feet of dirt, plot 329.

BENARD: You think six feet of dirt mean something?

LEON: Means whatever you was planning on doing in the world, ain't getting done.

BENARD: How many ways you think it is to be dead, boy?

LEON: That ain't the question, daddy. Question is how many ways is it to be here, *in* the world? Ain't got time for you. I come here trying to fix something 'tween me and my son.

BENARD: *(Laughing)* What in the hell *you* gone fix? I'm surprised you made it this far! Listen, let's not get started like this. I picked up my horn tonight, feel like playing. Thought about a piece of music, put me in the mind of that summer we spent breaking them geldings in the sandbars on the Arkansas River with your Uncle Travis?

LEON: We ain't spent no summers together.

BENARD: I spent more time fishing yo' ass out the Arkansas River than I spent—

LEON: You ain't fished me out of nothing.

BENARD: Don't matter how much you *think* you can swim. Once you actually in the river? It's a whole 'nother world.

LEON: Leave me the hell alone!

BENARD: Now see, this is how come I know you ain't gone make it. Ain't but one way for me to be here. *(He points to* LEON, *then takes out his flask and takes a nip.)* Was a time when Negroes was grateful to simply be breathing. Everything else was... "salt peanuts, salt peanuts..."

*(*BENARD *offers the flask to* LEON. LEON *stares at the flask but does not take it.* BENARD *takes another sip, it's empty.)*

BENARD: Damn.

*(*BENARD *exits.* MARCUS *returns. An echo of the phone again.* MARCUS *checks the phone, puts it back on the receiver. The ringing subsides.)*

LEON: *(To* MARCUS*)* I was here before. New York City. Back in '77. General Electric sent me.

MARCUS: I heard the story.

LEON: Been a while. I must'a forgot half of what we ever talked about.

MARCUS: Listen, I just got here, I'm starving and I don't feel like making nothing. I need to go out, pick up a few things.

LEON: Don't make no special trip for my sake.

MARCUS: Right. I need to go out right now. I'll bring you something back, case you get hungry.

LEON: I'm doing alright.

*(*BENARD *enters with the flask in hand, takes a sip. Offers to* LEON, *who puts his hand up, "no".)*

BENARD: Look like you *need* a little taste.

MARCUS: Fine.

BENARD: You ain't gone find no scotch with some age on it like this though.

*(*BENARD *holds out the flask again.* LEON *ignores him.)*

BENARD: Here I am trying to do a little something for you!

(Music slips out here.)

BENARD: Ain't that what you always crying about? What I ain't done for you?

*(*MARCUS *gets his coat and starts for the door. Leon checks his watch.)*

LEON: It's after midnight, but I was hoping to meet your wife.

MARCUS: She's taking a little time, back home. Said she needed family close by.

LEON: You ain't family?

MARCUS: Blood. Blood family.

LEON: Right. (*He moves to the "picture widow" that looks out over the city.*) Few times we talked you ain't told me 'bout your place. It's nice. Look like you can see the whole city from—

MARCUS: You know what, we should'a did this over the phone too.

LEON: Cain't do nothing for you over the phone, son.

MARCUS: What are you gonna *do* for me?

LEON: I figure if you cain't talk to your old man 'bout something like this then—

MARCUS: We talk about the weather, right? I say, how you doing and you give me a medical history I ain't really listening to 'cause I know half of your problem is what's in that leather pouch. I say, my wife is gone, you say, the place is nice. The carfare was no big thing, you're already here, what am I supposed to do? But I don't really have time for the kind of talking we do and I can't think of nothing I need you to do for me.

LEON: Your mouth. All right?

MARCUS: Do you even know my son's name?

LEON: You think I don't know I fucked up? Maybe I ain't got time to waste to make it right. My diabetes and my—

MARCUS: Oh. That's it. You wanna come here, feel good about yourself. Get some peace of mind 'cause your sugar's bad or who the hell knows what. My son has been missing for a week and I don't know where he is. Do you even understand what that means? (*He takes money out of his wallet and puts it on the table.*) Your room is the second door to the right. The kitchen is there. This is your car fare back to the airport. Tomorrow morning. Whatever it costs to change your

flight, I'll pay it. I don't want anything from you. I
don't need anything from you. Especially right now.

LEON: Now wait a—

MARCUS: Listen, I don't know how long it's been, but
you don't look so good. You know where it is if you
need it.

LEON: Look me in the eye and tell me what you think I
need. A man ought'a take a look at a thing for *hisself*.
Say what it is for *hisself*. No matter what my situation
was, no matter how bad I been down, I never asked
you to put yourself out for me. Never. *(Silence)* What's
the map for?

MARCUS: First couple of days I went to the same places,
saw the fliers I left the day before. Now, every street,
every block, every borough. I put a check, means I was
there, and Stephen was not.

LEON: These next couple of days, maybe I can—

MARCUS: Like I said, it's probably best you leave in the
morning. I'm waiting on a phone call. If it rings, let the
machine get it.

LEON: Least I can do is take a message for you.

MARCUS: If you don't mind. Let the machine get it.

*(*MARCUS *exits.* BENARD's *music kicks in with the horn.)*

BENARD: Ha! What you know 'bout that! Seattle, boy!
July 19 and 43. "Sammy's Underground Café." Joe
Wood on the bottom, Billy Jennings on the snare. Now
that's how we started the night.

LEON: How you talk my mother out to Seattle?

BENARD: Ain't had to say one word. She saw me
packing, she started packing.

LEON: 19 and 43. 'Bout the time Uncle Harold shipped
out—

BENARD: And come home with one eye! I tol' that Negro to get on the train, come to Seattle wit' me.

LEON: Maybe you should'a been wit'em, 'stead of dragging my mother to Seattle

BENARD: You got to go back to the beginning, to understand what me and Mugg had. But you don't wanna do that, do you?

LEON: You could'a been there for D-Day, the Battle of the Bulge, something.

BENARD: Know how we met? I was *running* through women, *still* ain't had the gumption to introduce myself. That's how fine yo' mama was. I say, "Harold, Mugg yo' cousin. You gonna make me beg you for an introduction?"

LEON: Maybe then you would'a floated up on one them beaches at the end of the day, maybe somebody identify the body.

BENARD: Harold say, "Mugg", that's what he nicknamed her, he say, "Mugg, this my partner Benard. His people's salt of the earth".

LEON: Least you could'a done something worth something.

BENARD: She say, "Salt? I don't generally use seasoning till *after* I taste my food. Sometimes not at all." That's what she said!

LEON: Least we'd a got the check. The check would'a did us some good.

BENARD: *(Stops playing abruptly)* A check? Negro please! Your draws come from Newmans, finest cuts of meat from the Stotlz Brothers on University Ave, hell you ate better than the president. We had an understanding, me and Mugg, you hear me? An understanding. I was a man of my time!

(Music kicks in around them, quick pace.)

BENARD: All right now! You hear that? *("Pointing" to the music)* What you think?

LEON: I don't think about nothing you ever said, nothing you ever did, nothing you ever was.

BENARD: Yeah you do, son. Hell, I'm pretty much all you think about.

(BENARD begins to play again, begins slow but the pace rises quickly. MARCUS enters and moves quickly to the kitchen. LEON stares from his son to his father. The horn is flying, a staccato burst and a high shriek and BENARD runs out of breath.)

BENARD: Whew! I could hurt somebody!

(MARCUS enters, takes off his jacket. LEON is staring at his father. MARCUS reaches for the phone.)

LEON: Ain't ring one time.

MARCUS: Got some Chinese noodles if you're hungry.

LEON: That's fine. I'm doing alright.

(MARCUS shrugs, sits down to eat.)

LEON: Probably ought'a eat something 'fore I take my shot. Anything with vegetables is good. Cain't do meat this time of the night. Makes me dream.

(MARCUS points to an unopened container. LEON tries to eat with the chopsticks.)

LEON: How the hell you eat with these damn things?

MARCUS: Forks in a drawer to the right of the sink.

LEON: Any salt in there?

MARCUS: On the counter.

LEON: Shouldn't be eating it, 'specially this time of night, but it's hard to put it down. *(Enters the kitchen)*

MARCUS: "What you love is your fate." Frank Bidart. Poet. Depressing cat. "Whether you love what you love or live in divided ceaseless revolt against it, what you love is your fate." Words.

LEON: *(Returns from the kitchen)* That don't seem possible if you got an ounce of common mother wit.

MARCUS: You can't always pick and choose when it comes to love. That's all the man is saying. Once you love a thing, that's what it is. Everything you do, don't do, all based on that love. That goes for a woman, for a child, even for salt.

LEON: I don't care how much love is in the room. One thing I know is how to leave somebody alone.

(LEON and MARCUS look at each other for a moment.)

MARCUS: Yep. Say you got that down.

LEON: When I think about how we got here, one thing I always say, that boy, he got his own mind. Ain't afraid to speak it. Course he liable to lose a few teeth in the process but there it is. I'm still proud of you. Kind'a glad I never sat you down, taught you nothing about how to be with a woman.

MARCUS: *(Laughs)* Everything I know about being with a woman, I got from you. All this time I was making it a point not to do anything I ever saw you do. Ain't that something?

LEON: Ain't that something.

(LEON rises to exit, stopped by BENARD who tries to blow his horn a few times but the note is off.)

BENARD: Damn! One thing I know after all these years, if the note don't come true, it ain't me.

LEON: I guess my mother was the one then, a bit off key, and I should'a been satisfied with draws from Newmans.

BENARD: You think 'cause I was in the street I ain't
felt nothing? Your mama only human being on earth
ever scared me. First time she kissed me I had to quit
gambling for a week! (*Pointing to his chest.*) I was all
opened up in here, Negroes see right through me.
Scared to blow my horn for fear it'd crack up my lips!
You ain't gone never understand how much I *thought*
about Mugg.

(YVETTE *enters. She straightens up here and there,
mindlessly, stacking magazines. She moves down to look out
at the city.*)

(MARCUS *stares at her.*)

LEON: When the last time a thought got up and loved
somebody?

(LEON *enters the kitchen.* BENARD *exits. Lights shift to
focus on* MARCUS *and* YVETTE. *The horn plays a light
melody through this, picking through the notes like walking
through a minefield.*)

YVETTE: This city is so small and so big all at the same
time. Everybody says that, right?

MARCUS: It's the people. It's a lot of people.

YVETTE: I took the #5 train into Brooklyn yesterday, the
express. Because Stephen, he could be anywhere, right?
After a while I forgot which train I was on, so I looked
at the map by the door—

MARCUS: And it don't really matter what time of the
day. A whole sea of people.

YVETTE: (*She indicates distance with fingers on one hand.*)
Maybe I looked lost because a little girl in the seat
next to me said, "Which train you looking for, Miss?"
Which was no help either...by then I'd forgotten where
I was going.

MARCUS: People are always looking at their feet or acting like they sleep or—

YVETTE: What good is a map if you don't know where you wanna go, if you don't have a plan? So I turned around and came home. It took me forever to climb these steps.

MARCUS: All these people and I swear nobody ever looks at you!

YVETTE: I felt so heavy. My shoes my bag my coat my keys…like I just swam across the ocean and crawled out soaking wet, heavy as a ton of bricks.

MARCUS: Not on the street, not on the train, not in this building, not one person has ever looked at me!

YVETTE: So I have decided not to eat for awhile. That might help. Right? A little hunger makes you… concentrate.

MARCUS: So tell me how in the world somebody *looks* at my boy?

YVETTE: A little mahogany boy with high cheeks? People don't see that everyday. If I saw him coming down the street, I would look at him. *(Silence)* What's your favorite color?

MARCUS: I don't know.

YVETTE: Pick one. Lie if you have to.

MARCUS: Then what does it matter?

YVETTE: Because sometimes a lie is a good thing, sweeter than the truest truth. Don't you tell all these beautiful lies to get to the truth when you write? "The story is not about reality, it is about truth." Isn't that what you say?

MARCUS: Blue.

YVETTE: Your favorite time of year?

MARCUS: Fall.

YVETTE: You remember that mudcloth scarf you wore when I first met you?

MARCUS: Of course.

YVETTE: You looked like…I don't know. I loved the way you looked. *(Silence)* We wanted to travel didn't we? So many places we wanted to go. You remember all the places we wanted to go?

MARCUS: Yvette, why are you asking me—?

YVETTE: 'Cause I need to tie things down. Don't you want to tie things down?

MARCUS: I don't see how this…yeah, lets tie it all down.

YVETTE: Your least favorite place?

MARCUS: Right here.

YVETTE: Excuse me?

MARCUS: I'm not doing this. All right? You want me to disappear? You wanna beat me? Here. Beat me till I disappear.

YVETTE: For me. Hmm? Do this for me.

MARCUS: War. That's the worst place I have ever been.

YVETTE: Did you kill anyone? I mean, while you there, in the Gulf?

MARCUS: Versus since I been home?

YVETTE: Well since you been home—

MARCUS: Stop. All right.

YVETTE: Yes. While you were there.

MARCUS: *(Laughs)* You said you never wanted to know. "I don't need to hear it if you don't want to say it." That's what you said.

YVETTE: Well things change, don't they. I heard Mister Schomburg down the hall ask you one afternoon and I thought how rude.

MARCUS: Mister Schomburg has numbers on his wrist, Yvette. Mister Schomburg really didn't want to know if I killed someone or how many I killed or how I killed them or anything about me at all. Mister Schomburg wanted to know something about *himself.* So what are you asking me?

YVETTE: I wanted to ask you this very question the moment I saw you step from the plane.

MARCUS: Then why didn't you?

YVETTE: Because you said you come home for this life, for children one day running around our feet and I needed, no, I *wanted* you to be the father you always said you couldn't wait to be not because I couldn't do it alone but 'cause I knew we could do it so much better together and all of that was much bigger than any one question or answer. But now, I can't help but think about what you did or didn't do because something *must* happen, something at the core of who you are, some door must open that never quite shuts, if you've killed somebody. Maybe I was more scared to hear it than you were to say it. I don't know. It's just that now...maybe that would explain this...maybe that would tie this one thing down for me, Marcus.

MARCUS: Explain what? What are we trying to tie down!

YVETTE: Something must have changed for you to let something like this...happen.

MARCUS: No. No no no. I'm not doing this for you, I didn't let this happen! You think I'm just sitting there watching some idiot walk off with our child? My son? You think...I mean, who the hell... Alright. Alright.

Okay. Here it is. I killed…people. And every time
I pulled the trigger I emptied the clip and I didn't
always know which ones were mine or somebody
else's but it doesn't really matter 'cause every time, I
was scared and happy as hell it was them and not me
who was dead because I wanted this life and I didn't
care what it cost. All right? Is that what you need to
know?

YVETTE: I thought I'd feel better. I should feel better.

MARCUS: Do you?

YVETTE: No. *(Pause)* But maybe you could do it again
and it would be easier. You could find whoever did
this and do it again. You could do that right?

MARCUS: You understand what you're asking me?

YVETTE: It could be kind of like something you'd write.
Yes? With the crazy glow of sunset in the background!

MARCUS: We can't do this, Vette, not like this.

YVETTE: We already *doing* this! We doing this till
Stephen comes through that door. You did this to
complete strangers who never did anything to you.
You did it for some figment of imagination called
Uncle Sam. Who the fuck is he! But you won't do it for
Stephen?

MARCUS: Yvette, that's not what I'm—!

YVETTE: Yvette? Who is that? I don't know who she
is. I'm walking through this house and breathing and
talking but this is not me. This is not my life.

MARCUS: What you want me to do?

YVETTE: I want my baby! I want you to leave out of
here and murder everybody you see till you find my
baby, Marcus, he is flesh and blood we made and I'm
telling you right now it is all right to murder the world
until he is home with me, with us. That's what I want.

MARCUS: That's what I'll do then, huh? Just like that. I'll get my coat and hat. I'll take some extra clothes and—

YVETTE: *(Looking at the people walking by below their window)* Look at them. People are just walking, up and down the street, buying groceries, going about their daily business. They have no idea that just above their heads there is nothing but *war!* Make this right, Marcus. You. You lost our son and you need to bring him back home! *(Pause)* Did you hear that?

MARCUS: No.

YVETTE: The phone? You didn't hear the phone?

MARCUS: He already called today. He's not calling again 'til tomorrow.

YVETTE: Maybe it's unplugged or—

MARCUS: We never unplug the phone, Vette. Never. You know that.

YVETTE: Are you sure? I mean are you really sure about anything in the whole damn world?

MARCUS: The man calls everyday.

YVETTE: You could check the connection.

MARCUS: One time everyday day.

YVETTE: Why don't you at least check the connection? That would seem to be the very least you could do. *(Beat)* Or am I asking for too much?

(YVETTE exits quickly. MARCUS rises to check the phone, listens for a dial tone. LEON enters.)

LEON: Seem like you get a little too much sugar, everything goes to hell. Bad feet, bad hands, pressure's bad. Runs in the family. My father, his father, Uncle Babe...might be something you wanna get checked.

(Beat) Month ago I had my doctor give me some Viagra, just in case.

MARCUS: In case of what?

BENARD: You cain't fault Goodwater for being good water.

LEON: You think I'm bad, your grandfather ain't met a woman he ain't took something from. If it whatn't money it was—

MARCUS: You ever listen to your father's music?

*(*MARCUS *pulls the 45 out of a basket and puts it on, a slow jazz groove.* BENARD *perks up.)*

LEON: He ain't made but one record I knew of, and it whatn't on the shelf but a minute.

MARCUS: I got it, right here. Found it on line. I'm looking for these old lullabies, searching everywhere and there he was. I'm looking at my grandfather's picture. Didn't even know he played, let alone cut a record.

LEON: Didn't even know you knew what he looked like.

BENARD: Knew there was something about that boy I liked.

LEON: *(He gets up.)* Marcus, I ain't really in the mood to hear that right now, you don't mind.

*(*MARCUS *takes the music off.* BENARD *exits.)*

LEON: That jazz stuff, never really was my thing. Might should'a saved your money, bought a few more of them lullabies instead.

MARCUS: I bought'em all. Every one I found. Still do.

*(*YVETTE *steps in from the hallway in her bare feet, wearing a slip. Silence.)*

LEON: May not look like it, when you think about how I been with the women in my life, but I do know a good love is a cure for whatever ails you.

(LEON *goes to the window. Lights shift.* BENARD'*s recording slips in.* MARCUS *is writing.*)

YVETTE: I just put Stephen down…sleep before he hit the pillow.

MARCUS: Long day.

YVETTE: He just goes and goes till he falls out.

MARCUS: Right. You sing to him?

YVETTE: Two words! *(Beat)* Still working?

MARCUS: A minute or—

YVETTE: I should go—

MARCUS: No baby.

YVETTE: Maybe I should change into…something…more…or less—

MARCUS: You know I dig you in that slip with them pretty feet of yours peeking out.

YVETTE: *(Teasing)* Then how long you gone make me stand here?

(MARCUS *opens his arms and* YVETTE *comes to him. They kiss.*)

YVETTE: I will always love your fingers in my hair, you breath behind my ears.

MARCUS: And I will always love that crazy little thing you do with your tongue!

YVETTE: Look at our life, Marcus. From three rooms and not one straight corner—

MARCUS: Paper thin walls, neighbors staring every time we step out the apartment.

YVETTE: What is a sister supposed to do? I swear, once, you turned the whole world purple, outside the window purple treetops, purple clouds, purple streets. How am I supposed to keep quiet when the whole world is turning purple?

MARCUS: I love you.

YVETTE: Every place you touch me—

MARCUS: I love you, baby.

YVETTE: Takes me someplace new.

MARCUS: You know that, right?

YVETTE: What I know is I'm standing here in a five dollar slip you love more than anything I own. You came home from a war in one piece. We made a beautiful, healthy little baby boy. And I am going to love you till it's all said and done. Nothing we can hold in our hands is ever going to be bigger than us.

MARCUS: You trying to work my game? You cain't work my game—

YVETTE: You ain't the only one in here know how to whisper sweet nothings.

MARCUS: I'm always holding a little somethin' somethin' in the back, keep you on your pretty little toes.

YVETTE: Try me.

MARCUS: Purple?

YVETTE: Ohhhh Marcus...there are so *many* colors in the world. Put that down and come to bed. Show me something new.

(YVETTE *backs away and* MARCUS *starts to follow. Lights shift.*)

LEON: This is what I remember 'bout New York. Streets full of people all night long.

MARCUS: *(Heads down to look out at the city)* So many colors. The trees along the streets, in the park. I think I seen every color Fall can bring and then I go out in the evening with Vette and Stephen and sunset comes in like a wash and every shade of green or blue slips to the left or the right and it's all brand new.

(BENARD enters, finishing the melody.)

LEON: Thought for sure she'd be here, your wife...how long she been gone?

MARCUS: A few days maybe, a week.

LEON: A man and a woman, even in the best of times, right?

BENARD: You ain't *never* gone *know* nothing 'bout what a real woman will do! A real woman is trickier than cards or horses or anything you can put odds on. She liable to hand you money with one hand and cut you with the other.

LEON: Hard, something like this. You just cain't say how a person will take it.

BENARD: Nothing beats a good understanding. *Nothing.*

LEON: *(To* MARCUS*)* Nobody ever said loving was easy.

MARCUS: Seem like loving ought to be the easiest thing ever made, easier than breathing, easier than living.

(Lighting shift, a spot maybe, and YVETTE *comes on with her coat and gloves and scarf, and suitcase. She comes down to the picture window that looks out over the city. She is putting on her coat and scarf and gloves.)*

YVETTE: I left my mother's number by the bed.

MARCUS: I know the number.

YVETTE: I'm going to say good-bye now.

MARCUS: I'm trying to tie this down, Vette. I'm going out there every day trying to tie this down.

YVETTE: Please, Marcus. I tried too. You call me when there's news.

MARCUS: *(To* LEON*)* I thought she'd go home, take a minute, come to the fact we need each other, she'd come back and "say all right, Marcus. All right. *We* can do this."

YVETTE: It doesn't matter where I go, to the market to the...I always come back here. And Stephen is not here.

MARCUS: Together, Vette... That's how we survive this 'til the phone rings and he tells us what we want to hear.

YVETTE: I need to get out of the city. That's it. Everyday it's always more of the same. Don't call if it's the same. Please.

MARCUS: Together is what keeps us sane in the midst of frogs and blood falling out the sky, and just 'cause that ain't possible don't mean it won't happen, but we built a life on this rock between us, didn't we? That's what you say to the one you lay down with when you give up that thing that makes you...you put it in their hands and say what I got for you is beyond love baby I got crazy *trust* that you will guard this like the fifth battalion and you give me yours and I will keep it like the Alamo and no man made or natural disaster or otherwise can take this gift you gave me, nothing but a decree from God and we ain't even no where close to being in a position to hear *anything* from God personally...we just here for each other...and we might even go toe to toe with God if it gets funky enough but that's how it is when you love. Yvette please. Hate me. If you cain't do nothing else, hate me. But stay. Please.

YVETTE: I don't know, Marcus. I don't know anything. I see my sister pulling up. I don't want to keep her waiting. *(She is bundling up. She is missing a glove.)* I cannot keep a pair of gloves to save my life!

MARCUS: Nothing is ever going to be bigger than us. I know you remember that.

YVETTE: Every time I close my eyes I see the deep grain of his skin, Marcus, I can't help it, the dark lines curving around his cheeks, down to his little belly button, shooting out to his little hands. *(Beat)* My sister... She's come all this way.

MARCUS: Maybe I should come, for a few days and—

YVETTE: One of us should stay here. Don't you think? Why don't you stay here. *(She exits.)*

MARCUS: Till it's all said and done. People say that all the time, don't they?

LEON: Maybe you ought not wait for her to call. Maybe you should go on and call her.

MARCUS: It's the detective. He should'a called by now.

LEON: Kind of late.

MARCUS: He calls everyday 'tween three and four o'clock. Said he wouldn't sleep till he got to the end of this, said he'd call whether it was something or nothing, and that's what it's been, nothing, and everyday he calls to say it. But not today.

LEON: Been two weeks. Your granny told me—

MARCUS: You 'member Colombo? That's what he looks like. I swear, the coat the cigar the bad eye Peter Faulk had, the whole thing. You 'member that show? Who the hell is he looking at with that eye? You know that's what the criminal was saying, "Is he looking at me with that eye?" And Colombo was always cool, right?

MARCUS/LEON: "Just one thing I don't understand, just one thing I was hoping you could help me out with"—

MARCUS: And then you knew you was about to be locked up. I met him a couple years ago, Peter Faulk. He was doing an Arthur Miller play downtown. I had a hook up, went back stage after the show. I was co-chairing this benefit and we needed a name, thought we could trick him into coming, give him a prize or something.

LEON: You get him?

MARCUS: Naw. Saw right through me, but he was cool about it. Told him I really dug Colombo. He said the work schedule was brutal, some weeks they'd be down to the last day of filming for the week and the writers still hadn't figured out who did the murder, sometimes he'd have to come up with some shit right on the spot. That's crazy right. I mean do you know how many wrong cats is sitting in tv prison right now 'cause the writers ran out of time and Colombo had to make up some shit on the spot? Soon as I met this detective, I knew...Colombo ain't worth a damn without a good writer.

LEON: Probably wouldn't mind a call. Something important as this.

(YVETTE *enters in the same dress as the top of the play and is still.*)

MARCUS: "We're exhausting all the avenues, double checking every lead, time is the enemy, some small moment that comes to mind, they pop up just like that sometimes, a little detail slipped your mind in the initial chaos, like for instance where the hell were you when your child went missing in the first place!

(Quick lighting shift)

YVETTE: What do you mean, you don't know. How can you not know, Marcus, where Stephen is? *(Silence)* Baby. Please.

MARCUS: We looked for three hours, me, the police, damn near everybody in the park, we looked at every inch of that park again and again and again— *(Silence)*

I took my journal this morning. I took it cause I was writing, earlier, and it was all in my head and I was trying to get on the page, so I took the journal. We got a cab so we could get there quick, Stephen was ready to play. We hit the ice cream truck first, then the jungle gym, Dante was there, I had my journal but I… soon as he heard the music at the merry-go-round we went straight there. You know how he…I put him on a horse. I buckled him up. I watched him go round and round, I mean I, I opened my journal for a minute, you know, to get it back, I swear it was just a minute and then all of the sudden—

(Through the rest of this YVETTE *is shaking her head "no" and saying "no" until that is all that can be heard. In this, her "no" should be the last note of this.)*

MARCUS: —there was no music and I didn't see Stephen right away, not right away but I, I went around three times I, I checked every horse, I looked underneath, Vette I swear I just looked down for a minute, I just looked down for a minute…I just—

(End of music. Silence)

MARCUS: The detective is coming here. To talk to us.

YVETTE: To us? He's coming to talk to *us*? I wasn't there. But you were. His father. Right? You were there.

*(*YVETTE *exits.)*

(Lighting shift)

LEON: He'll call. Time gets away from people, hell you get old and—

MARCUS: This is not gone work. All right?

LEON: Lets just get through this first. Then maybe—

MARCUS: I got issues with you that I can't deal with right now.

LEON: I know but listen—

MARCUS: Laughing about the few good days we had ain't gone fix it.

LEON: Just let me help you through—

MARCUS: Maybe on some level I really do wanna laugh and joke with you, daddy—

BENARD: The boy ought to make *his self* in the world, like we all made ourselves in the world generation upon generation! Ain't nobody crying 'bout, "where was you?"

MARCUS: —maybe break down and cry in front of my old man—

BENARD: I don't know why you never understood that.

MARCUS: But I can't.

BENARD: I know what you wanna hear—

MARCUS: I'm looking in my child's face everyday and swearing to be a better man, a better father than you—

BENARD: You wanna hear "I'm sorry, I should'a been there—

LEON: *(To* BENARD*)* A minute of peace!

MARCUS: —swearing I'd never leave never quit never let hurt harm or danger come to him without me giving up the ghost and I'm still standing here, warm blood in my veins, and Stephen ain't here!

BENARD: What make you think I owe you something?!

MARCUS: I look into the mirror and the lines around my eyes belong to you! Every *day* it's like you coming out of my pores and I can't do nothing about it.

LEON: I understand, Marcus. But we still got to have something left between us. You and me.

(Everything stops.)

LEON: I know it don't seem possible. But that's how we began.

MARCUS: You not hearing me. You didn't get on that plane today for me or my son. You got on that plane for you.

LEON: I come here 'cause I know what this is, son. To be in the middle of the river and you too damn tired to swim any way but down. And I thought maybe I could—

MARCUS: What? Help me? Look at you.

(LEON *is shaking almost out of his chair,* BENARD *takes out his flask, takes a nip and offers some to* LEON. LEON *refuses.* BENARD *takes another nip. The notes hang lush and languid.)*

LEON: When you first come in the world, you whatn't but this big, so yellow the doctor thought you had the jaundice but I knew you ain't done nothing but reached back a few generations to your great granddaddy. I saw generations from the grave to the cradle, standing there, holding you in the crook of my arm, your mama laying there spent, so it was on me to be there for you. That's right. On me. I swear to you, Marcus, that was the first time I ever really felt like a man. All the fooling around on your mama, that foolishness that got me sent to prison… Nothing ever come close to that moment! What it was to be a man. To be a father. That's how we began.

MARCUS: I can't be in this place and get my help from you.

LEON: Son, at some point, everybody is wrong. That cain't be the end of it!

MARCUS: You think one night, a couple of days, you can come here and erase years?

LEON: All I'm saying is that a man, some point in his life, ought to try to do right. That's all I'm trying to do.

(Beat)

MARCUS: (Shaking his head "no".) I need to put the food away.

(MARCUS exits into the kitchen.)

(BENARD holds out the flask towards LEON. LEON hesitates then takes it and quickly throws back drink. He quickly hands it back to BENARD.)

BENARD: Hard head make a soft ass.

LEON: I swear I come here for Marcus and his boy.

BENARD: Harold come home from the war trying to tell me how right I better be with Mugg. I said, Harold, right is a relative thing. Look here, the U S Army sent you home from a war with a bowl cut and a glass eye, and they still sat yo' ass at the back of the train! Now that ought to tell you the whole damn world is wrong and you got to make it best you can.

LEON: I swear that's why I come here.

BENARD: You hear the boy say it-ain't-gone-work? When you think about it, when the last time you tried something that actually worked? And you cain't put that on nobody but you.

(BENARD begins to play here, a staccato burst and LEON winces as if his head is about to explode.)

LEON: I'm getting real tired of that horn.

(MARCUS enters.)

MARCUS: It's almost three in the morning. Maybe you should—

LEON: (He is on the verge of tears.) Naw, I'm fine. I'm fine. I just need a minute, you know, 'fore I lay down. My sugar is probably a little off 'cause I got started

so early this morning and then the airport, the damn
airport, they checks your bags like you was some kind
of a criminal you believe they made me take off my
damn shoes! What is a grown man gonna hide in his
shoes!

MARCUS: First door on the right. Your bag is in there.

LEON: Right. Right. Little sleep. You right. That's all I
need. I be fine.

(MARCUS *turns to exit down the hallway.*)

LEON: Marcus.

(MARCUS *turns.*)

LEON: You put everything in the room?

BENARD: "Salt peanuts, salt peanuts…"

MARCUS: Your coat your bag, your…oh. That's not
what you're asking me about, right?

(MARCUS *pulls the small leather pouch out of the drawer.*)

(BENARD *continues to hum the melody through this.*)

MARCUS: Must have slipped my mind, all the
excitement, reminiscing 'bout the good ol' days and
whatnot.

(MARCUS *lays the pouch down in front of his father.* LEON
*is transfixed now, his head in his hands, staring at the
pouch.* MARCUS *mimics* LEON.)

MARCUS: 'Cause a man, a man ought to try not to *stay*
wrong. A man ought to take a look at a thing for *hisself.*
Say what the truth of it really is.

(*A moment passes.* LEON *staring at the package,* MARCUS
staring at LEON, BENARD *staring out to eternity. After a
moment* MARCUS *turns to exit up the hallway.*)

(*The phone rings. It rings forever.*)

(MARCUS *answers.*)

MARCUS: Hello…

(Blackout)

END OF ACT ONE

ACT TWO

(Light comes up dim on the scene; BENARD, *singing to himself, his horn dismantled once again, his socks and shoes off, his suit coat hanging off the back of his chair, his shirt out, his pork pie hat on the back of his chair. He is wiping his forehead and face with his handkerchief, rubs his feet.* LEON *is sitting, wrapping himself up in his own arms, but he is having great difficulty remaining still.* MARCUS *is still standing, holding the phone. After a moment, lighting up on* BENARD.)

BENARD: To tell the truth, which most folk don't wanna hear, ain't really no such thing as love or hate. I know that's a hard fact to swallow, like day old crow, but that's one thing I won't do and that's lie about what's real. Anything worth its' weight in the world comes down to one simple thing, a good understanding. And a good understanding is based on facts, agreed on facts. Right from jump street, this is what you gotta do, this is where you gotta be, this is how you got to operate. You ain't got that kind of understanding? All manner of hell is subject to creep in on you. What is love? Anybody tell you they know…is a natural born fool. Tell somebody to spell out "love," and that's as close as you ever gone get to knowing what the hell "love" is. Trust me when I tell you all of my troubles come from a lack of understanding.

(Lights up on MARCUS *with the phone. He hangs it up slowly. A lighting shift and* YVETTE *is just inside the*

entrance to the apartment. She is bundled in a heavy coat and scarf and gloves. Her eyes are closed.)

YVETTE: Marcus, can I open my eyes now?

MARCUS: Just a minute.

*(*MARCUS *"shakes" away the phone call, goes to* YVETTE *and brings her down to the window.)*

YVETTE: This is crazy! You wake me up at five in the morning, bring to who knows where, make me close my eyes like we're in the fifth grade, I am tired and sleepy and—

MARCUS: Open.

YVETTE: Where are we?

MARCUS: I want you to see sunrise from here.

YVETTE: Sunrise? *(Beat)* Marcus—

MARCUS: Just went on the market yesterday, the Realtor noticed me from my book, let me hold the key, for a deposit.

YVETTE: A deposit, Marcus?

MARCUS: Just for the key. That's all. We can get it back, I mean, if you don't like it...I just didn't want to take a chance, if you like it—

YVETTE: I love it. *(She comes out of the outer wear as she moves about the room and finally to the window.)*

MARCUS: You do? You really do?

YVETTE: I do, but, I mean, look at this view, Marcus, I never thought I would, "we" would...can we?

MARCUS: I went straight from the publisher to the bank and the check passed. Yeah.

YVETTE: Your book is going to sell, baby. It's already selling.

MARCUS: You're right. We can do this. Together.

YVETTE: Is that the—? This is a big step, Marcus. Everything is moving so fast. You've only been home six months and already the publishers, the book launch, the...I mean from a fourth walk up to this... What if we—

(MARCUS *puts a finger to his mouth to quiet her.*)

I know. All right. I'm just... Oh my God. Sunrise standing here is going to be unbelievable. We need to have a dinner, right now, tomorrow, everybody we love, all our friends. Celebrate.

MARCUS: Can we get something to sit on in here first?

YVETTE: I know, right. I'm crazy! I'm just feeling crazy right now, loving life, loving you.

MARCUS: We get something to sit on in here—

YVETTE: Invite everybody we know—

MARCUS: Not everybody, 'cause the last thing we need is your drunk brother breaking—

YVETTE: You can stop talking 'bout my brother any minute now.

MARCUS: Good food, good wine, good friends.

YVETTE: This window is huge.

MARCUS: The city is...right here.

YVETTE: This doesn't open, right? I love this, Marcus, but I mean, if we have a child it has to be safe.

MARCUS: Yvette, it's a plate glass window from the ceiling to the floor. No. It doesn't open.

YVETTE: I'm crazy, I know, I'm just saying...you're home, a new place, new...everything good is... happening. You would do that though, right? Make it safe if—?

MARCUS: *We* would do that. You brother's drunk butt is liable to try to walk right through the window but—

YVETTE: I'm serious now. We cain't even count how many ways we are lucky to even be standing here, together. Six months ago you were standing on a street corner in Baghdad.

MARCUS: I did my bit for Uncle Sam. That's it. I'm home, baby.

YVETTE: When life is good like this, I just get a little scared.

MARCUS: We gone be everything we got to be, for us, for our baby, whenever he or she gets here. I'm right here. And pretty soon, this will be our home. Yes?

YVETTE: Yes.

(MARCUS and YVETTE *kiss and hug tightly. Teasing*)

YVETTE: You still want a baby?

MARCUS: Please. Yesterday! How many times we talk about this?

YVETTE: Before you left, everyday. It's just—

MARCUS: Ain't nothing changed… Ohhhhh, I see what it is, you wanna go 'head and get started *inaugurating* the rooms, right?

YVETTE: Stop playing.

MARCUS: I ain't playing!

YVETTE: *(She steps back.)* I do have something to tell you. I was gonna tell you in the morning, but here we are. Good friends, good food, all of that is cool. But good wine? I can't do that for a while.

MARCUS: What you mean you…?

YVETTE: Six weeks, Marcus. I'm six weeks.

MARCUS: No!

YVETTE: Yes!

MARCUS: Yes? A baby, you...? Six weeks...? Damn, we got a baby coming, we got a baby? You and me? Damn! When you—?

YVETTE: Yesterday. I mean, I took a home test last week but—

MARCUS: You been knowing for a week?

YVETTE: I wanted to be sure. Wrapped the box in three bags before I threw it away so you wouldn't see it. Went to see Doctor Phillips yesterday. He said six weeks. A little more, a little less. But...six weeks.

MARCUS: Ah Vette! Damn. I love you. This is...forget the windows, I'm double checking everything in here, everything! Code, everything baby proof, nah nah wait, cain't baby proof the world, right? They got to take a few scrapes here and there but they need to take'em right here, at home, they got to learn, right, they got to, damn. A baby. *(He puts his ear on her stomach.)* Whew.

(MARCUS jumps back as if he has just been kicked and they both laugh.)

YVETTE: Quit messing. *(She points out to the sunrise.)* Look. It's almost sunrise. The three of us, you and me and...baby, we are going to stand right here and watch the sunrise, in our soon to be new home. Can you believe it? *(She teases.)* I'm so glad you're home. Did I say that all ready?

MARCUS: Everyday for the last six months.

YVETTE: *(She starts to move about the space.)* What are we going to do with all of this space, Marcus?

MARCUS: Vette?

(MARCUS is looking out the window onto the city.)

MARCUS: You testing me? Right? Asking me if I still want a child, wrapping the home test in three bags and—

YVETTE: I just wanted to be sure.

MARCUS: About the baby? Or about me?

YVETTE: Marcus—

MARCUS: Because before I left for Iraq, we both talked about how much we wanted a family.

YVETTE: But we never talked about what you seen or didn't see, what you did or didn't do over there. What's different.

MARCUS: This life is what I came home for.

YVETTE: I know but you hear it on the news all the time. People come home, and they're not the same, maybe in some small way they don't even realize…and it's not even their fault.

MARCUS: You right. But everything I did, every time I thought I was about to go mad looking at some… at what a human being could do to another human being, I closed my eyes and thought about you, our child, our life together. I thought, this place is death but what I have with Yvette is life. Iraq was just a moment, right? I can't live in that moment and have a life. It doesn't work that way.

YVETTE: You trying to work my game? You know you cain't work my game. (Beat) People need time, sometimes. I understand.

MARCUS: I don't want to waste another minute. I'm in a hurry to be a good man, a good husband, a good father, the kind my daughter or my son would be proud of. Iraq can't change that.

YVETTE: I was scared, for just a minute, when I saw the blue line on the home kit.

MARCUS: *(He puts his finger to her lips to quiet her.)* I'm scared too, sometimes for no good reason, just scared. But you and me, we gonna love this baby like nobody's business. I can't wait.

YVETTE: Well you're gonna have to. At least seven more months. Show me the rest.

(MARCUS smiles and moves to follow YVETTE as she exits and is stopped by the glove she left behind.)

MARCUS: Vette, this is why you have a drawer full of miss-matched...gloves...Vette?

(MARCUS turns up and YVETTE is gone. He places the glove in the side table drawer. Lighting shift.)

LEON: *(He points to the leather pouch on the coffee table.)* Why don't you put that back where you got it from. Please.

MARCUS: Listen, if you need it, you need it.

LEON: I'll put it back my damn self!

MARCUS: I got it. *(He gets the pouch and puts it back in the same drawer with the glove.)*

BENARD: "Salt peanuts, salt peanuts..."

LEON: *(Ignoring BENARD. To MARCUS)* Look like you got some news. The phone call.

MARCUS: It was nothing.

BENARD: Trying to tell you to mind yo' own business.

LEON: The detective fella.

MARCUS: I know who you talking about.

LEON: That was him on the phone, right? Thought he might'a had some news for you, reason he called so late.

MARCUS: I said it was nothing.

LEON: Probably ought's get some sleep, but the sun'll be up soon, might as well stay on up.

MARCUS: Suit yourself.

(MARCUS *moves to the window.*)

BENARD: Thought you knew how to leave folk alone.

LEON: *(To* BENARD*)* That why you was screaming for Mugg not to leave at the train station in Seattle? 'Cause you know how to leave folk alone?

BENARD: Don't you ever talk to me about Seattle! You don't know the first thing 'bout Seattle.

MARCUS: *(Referring to the drugs)* I'm sorry about that. Should'a left it alone from the start.

LEON: Ain't no thing. Big ass elephant in the room. Something had to be said and I, well.. *(Beat).* You don't mind me asking, how you meet your wife?

(YVETTE *enters, wiping makeup off her face, walks D S past* MARCUS. *She is wearing a cat suit and high heels.* MARCUS *is speaking to* LEON, *but watching* YVETTE.)

MARCUS: We met at Columbia University. Angela Davis was speaking. Place was packed but I saw Vette across the lobby and I said to myself, if she goes to the reception, I'm going to the reception.

(YVETTE *winces in the shoes and finally takes them off, relief.)*

MARCUS: We talked a bit. I walked her home. Three blocks took three hours. Next morning I slipped a poem under her door, left my number on it, little note about a cup of coffee. She said, "I'd like that." Three little words tore me down. "I'd like that."

(Light change)

YVETTE: You didn't like the party.

MARCUS: You know, it was, it was a...no.

YVETTE: I didn't think so.

MARCUS: A bunch of grown folk dressed up in—

YVETTE: *(Teasing)* It was a Halloween party, Marcus. How you wanna be a writer? With so little imagination.

MARCUS: Oh I got plenty imagination, but your friend with the flamingo thing? Who wanna imagine what she gone be doing in that later on tonight? Naw. You looked good though.

YVETTE: You like my cat suit?

MARCUS: The cat suit is nice. But the shoes? Oh my, my, my. Yeah, I like that.

YVETTE: Now isn't that strange, you like the thing that caused me the most pain! These shoes 'bout to kill me!

MARCUS: Come on. Put your feet up here.

(YVETTE puts a foot in his lap and he begins to massage them..)

YVETTE: Shoes made my feet sweat…a little. They stink, don't they?

MARCUS: Yep.

(YVETTE tries to snatch her foot off MARCUS's lap, but he stops her.)

Never been afraid of a little funk. Relax. Let me do this.

YVETTE: Marry me.

MARCUS: *(He laughs.)* Let me jump up right now, two in the morning, and find a preacher.

YVETTE: I don't need a preacher or a church or a ring or anything. Marry me.

MARCUS: Quit playing.

YVETTE: I'm not playing.

(Beat)

MARCUS: *(Small laughter)* Baby, it's been what, three, four weeks?

YVETTE: How much time you need?

*(*MARCUS *is no longer laughing.)*

MARCUS: Are you...? Yvette. Look at me. Only reason I didn't wear a costume is 'cause I couldn't afford the three dollars to get one. Everything I got is sitting right here. You see how I'm holding onto this foot for dear life. I might need a little something to snack on later.

*(*MARCUS *and* YVETTE *both laughing.)*

MARCUS: Baby, ten years in the Navy and lucky they ain't kicked me out yet. I got a beat up car, a closet for an apartment. Don't have a dime to my name. Rather write a poem than eat.

YVETTE: How you think you got in here in the first place? I love it when you write, what you write. You should see yourself when you're writing. You get this little wrinkle in the middle of your forehead, which is cute, but kind of big too.

MARCUS: The wrinkle?

YVETTE: No. Your forehead. Oh don't be like that, my uncle Garcia has the biggest forehead in three states and he's the smartest man I know.

MARCUS: That's nice for your uncle but this...little wrinkle ain't helped me write nothing that's paying a bill. This is it. No master plan, nothing put away for the future. Nothing. All I got is a big...forehead...well, that ain't all I got.

*(*YVETTE *hits* MARCUS *softly, playfully.)*

MARCUS: And you want to marry me?

YVETTE: This is the first time I ever been loved like this. And I know it.

MARCUS: I told you 'bout mixing red wine and gin in the same night, you got to keep that mess separate.

YVETTE: You love me, Marcus?

(Beat)

MARCUS: Only thing I know.

YVETTE: How 'bout this. Lets go to bed. In the morning, write another poem for me. Wrap it in something nice. Then take me somewhere and marry me. I want to start my new life right now, but I can wait 'til sunrise.

MARCUS: All right. I can do that.

YVETTE: See there. Already. A plan.

(MARCUS and YVETTE laugh big, hug, kiss and she starts to exit.)

MARCUS: Listen, you think you can get into them shoes one mo' time tonight, I mean, just for a hot minute?

YVETTE: A hot minute?

MARCUS: Or two—

YVETTE: I don't know. Bring your big...fo'head on. I'll see what a sister can do for you. *(She starts to exit.)*

MARCUS: Yvette. Don't leave, alright. Stay here.

YVETTE: Just give me a minute to—

MARCUS: Can we just live in this moment? Just like this. For a little while?

YVETTE: That's not the way it works, silly. If we stay in this moment we won't get married in the morning, we won't have a family, we won't have a life. Don't you want a *life* together?

MARCUS: I do. More than anything. I want a life. With you. Together.

(YVETTE comes back to kiss MARCUS and then exits. He starts to follow and is stopped short by LEON's voice.)

LEON: Junction City! I know I never told you 'bout this. Standing outside a little joint for a minute, seen yo' mama riding by with your Grandpa in his ol' beat up truck.

MARCUS: And you knew it then?

LEON: Knew something. Cain't tell you exactly what it was though. Her daddy had a reputation for strangling cats if they looked for too long and I was sho'nuff staring, so you know it had to be something.

MARCUS: You must have done something right, least for the minute you was together.

LEON: Lucky we lasted that long. Yo' mama forever trying to kill me or get me killed.

MARCUS: That's not quite how I heard it. I heard it was women around every corner, panties and bras in the backseat of the car and—

LEON: Yeah well every story got a little more to it than what you get in the telling and it don't matter who's telling it. That's how I know it was me you was talking about. *(Beat)* That's right. I read your book. Surprised ain't you? Your Aunt told me about it and I got myself to one of those big book stores and found it. Whatn't hard. They had it set up in it's own little space and I said I'll be damn! Look at my boy. I was so damn proud. And they wouldn't even let me pay for it. I had the money. But I told'em you was my boy, pulled out your picture from when you was in the service. *(He takes the picture out of his wallet.)* The manager came over and gave me a copy. Just like that. Couldn't even wait till I got to the house to read it, I was trying to look at in the car. Drove all up on the damn curb. You know the last book I read? Hell I cain't even remember what it was. *(Beat)* I know that was me you was writing about.

MARCUS: Maybe that's what it started out to be, this thing between fathers and sons but—

LEON: That was me you wrote. First word fell out of the man's mouth, I knew it. And I knew I had to do something, between me and you, 'cause everything you said about me, I said about my daddy. Everything I hated about that man, I seen it in me, seem like for the first time, with that book in my hand. I said right then, my son ain't burying me feeling like I felt about my daddy. But I couldn't put the stuff down and it damn sho' whatn't putting me down. I swear I stayed straight that whole time you was in Iraq, read John 3:16 every morning for you son. And the day I heard you was coming home I thought, a little taste, to celebrate, might be alright and…When your Aunt told me about your boy, that he was missing, I knew it was time, do something worth something, help you any way I could.

(Silence. BENARD comes in with the horn. The notes are nice and tight. LEON is looking at MARCUS's military picture.)

LEON: You took a good picture. Kind of surprised me though. You in the service.

MARCUS: Surprised me too.

LEON: How the hell you in Navy and get sent to Iraq? I thought you was supposed to be on a boat or a—

MARCUS: Ships. No boats in the Navy. And I was an M P. M Ps and corpmen, always on the ground.

LEON: I'm just glad you come home in one piece.

MARCUS: Yeah. Me too.

(YVETTE enters here in a slip, carrying a portable phone and moves down to the "window" looking out over the city, holding herself tight.)

MARCUS: Ain't nothing like you think it's gone be. First couple times, mortar rounds come in, I just laid low. Scared. But then I put Vette's face in front of me, thought damn I love that woman and I *married* her, and maybe it's a little selfish to want something that bad that ain't even promised to you but I wanted *this*, I wanted my turn to be a father. I never quit being scared, but after that, I shot everything that even looked like it wanted to shoot me.

(The phone rings and YVETTE *quickly answers.)*

YVETTE: Marcus?

MARCUS: *(From where he is sitting)* Yeah. It's me.

YVETTE: There was nothing on the news for two days. When there's nothing on the news I worry, when there's news I worry. No news is good news, that's what they say, but it doesn't feel good, not knowing, it doesn't feel…I worry…Marcus, you still there?

MARCUS: I'm here.

YVETTE: I'm just talking away. You're back on base or the zone or the—

MARCUS: Yeah.

YVETTE: And everybody's fine?

MARCUS: I'm fine.

YVETTE: Nothing happened?

MARCUS: I'm good.

YVETTE: You went where you had to go you did what you had to do and you're back now and everybody is fine?

MARCUS: Baby we…yeah, everybody is all right—

YVETTE: And you won't have that duty again? You won't have to—

MARCUS: Vette, I gotta go where ever they tell me to go.

YVETTE: I'm just saying, Marcus.

MARCUS: And I'm just saying… *(Beat)* I'm good. I'm fine.

YVETTE: I know you're fine. I said that from across a lobby full of people, he's so fine. I'm gonna marry him, forehead and all!

MARCUS: Now see, it's late in New York, must be late, trying to throw a little rap on me, you know you cain't rap—

YVETTE: I knew you'd call.

MARCUS: I miss you. I love you.

YVETTE: You so crazy. You better love me! *(Beat)* Listen you will never believe what my brother got his self into—

MARCUS: Yes I would—

YVETTE: Do you know how many times I have sent him money and he still—?

MARCUS: I lost count, but he know how many times and that's exactly why he keeps calling!

YVETTE: Anyway, I told my mother this is the last time I'm dealing with him, and I know you remember Mr. Schomberg from down the hall, he is so nice- oh, you will never guess who called for you yesterday.

MARCUS: Who?

YVETTE: Guess.

MARCUS: Mickey Mouse.

YVETTE: See you play too much. The publisher, Marcus! The publisher.

MARCUS: He did not!

YVETTE: Yes! He said he loved the first draft and they want to talk to you about an editor and some other stuff I have written down, but they want to talk to you! I told him you was otherwise *occupied* and when you got home you would be otherwise *engaged* for a hot minute, or two—

MARCUS: A hot minute?

YVETTE: *(She begins to exit on this.)* Please, you'll be lucky to last that long when I put this on you, but trust me, you'll work up to something respectable in no time, none of which I said to the poor man, but he sounded so excited made me excited, and Marcus let me tell you...

(YVETTE continues talking and the light shifts as she exits.)

MARCUS: You were right about sunrise. Any minute now it's gonna happen and you don't wanna miss it. The first night Yvette saw the place, we stood right here, saw this same sunrise. All kinds of colors bleeding across the horizon. That's what it looks like, bleeding. Vette is standing here with all these colors moving over her and every color is something personal to her, like she feels them on her skin. For a while, after Stephen was born, she would stand right here every morning and cry, both of'em crying over the sky.

(BENARD enters.)

LEON: *("Looking" at BENARD)* I don't even need it.

MARCUS: What?

LEON: What's in that drawer. Don't even want it. I mean it. We ought'a flush it right now.

(BENARD grunts. LEON moves to the stand, opens the drawer, sees the gun and holds it up.)

LEON: What you planning on doing something with this?

MARCUS: *(He takes the gun, puts it back in the drawer, takes out the leather pouch and closes the drawer.)* I'll take care of this. *(He exits to the bathroom.)*

LEON: *(To* BENARD*)* Loving somebody is scary, right? And don't even talk about somebody loving you back. You must have been scared to death, the kind of love my mother had for you.

BENARD: Only reason Mugg caught that train out of Seattle was a lack of understanding. Ain't had nothing to do with love or—

LEON: You put together all of the lines of coke I have drawn out in the past twenty years, they run together like tributaries running into the Arkansas river, so many tides and eddies and undercurrents, so many ways to drown.

BENARD: *(Laughing off the fear)* Look here, when the dust clears, you gone be what you come in the world to be.

LEON: And all this time I been thinking, if you had'a just been there, for something, I'd be alright.

BENARD: And you cain't put that on me!

LEON: You're right. For years I been putting it on you.

(MARCUS enters.)

LEON: But I see it now and you ain't nowhere in the picture.

(BENARD exits. YVETTE enters in a summer dress. She moves past MARCUS into the kitchen and back out again. She moves to the drawer, takes out a pen and paper to write her shopping list. Marcus watches this happen.)

YVETTE: *(Finishing the list, speaking up the hallway)* Mommy's leaving, Stephen! *(To* MARCUS*)* I'm sorry. I know you wanna get to the park so you can get back here to write, but I told him he could pick his jacket.

MARCUS: That's fine, I can take some...notes.

YVETTE: I should have never said—

MARCUS: He's coming. It's all right. I mean, he's back there, looking for a jacket and—

YVETTE: He's your son, you know he's going to be forever. At this rate I'll be home from the market 'fore you two even get out the door. He's just like you.

MARCUS: What you mean?

YVETTE: Baby you know I love you but it takes you a half a day to pick out a pair of socks, and color matching, not your thing.

MARCUS: A jacket is a big thing when you're four, all kind of pre-schoolers on the block he got to watch out for. Stephen and me, we just a little particular about some things.

YVETTE: I give the child good looks, and you give the poor child—

MARCUS: Nothing wrong with being a little particular about some things. He's coming.

YVETTE: All right Stephen, Dante's mommy called and said they're already at the park, Dante is sliding and climbing the wall and— *(Whispers to* MARCUS*)* What else?

MARCUS: *(Whispers)* Ice cream—

YVETTE: Ice cream? Marcus, do not feed my child mess all day long.

MARCUS: Vette. Come on now. We going to the park, baby. One ice cream.

*(*YVETTE *eyes* MARCUS.*)*

MARCUS: One.

YVETTE: *(To Stephen down he hall)* Mommy's leaving, honey! Have fun at the park!

(MARCUS *starts down the hallway.*)

YVETTE: Do not go back there to help him. You two will never get out of here. And if you get yourself back here at a decent hour you won't have to settle for…ice cream.

MARCUS: Come on, Vette. Middle of August, it's hot, the park—

YVETTE: Ahhh baby. Am I asking for too much? Hmm? Am I asking for too much?

(YVETTE *taps* MARCUS *playfully on the arm and kisses him. She exits.*)

MARCUS: *(He moves up stage to look "up" the hallway. He picks up and checks to make sure his backpack has the "park necessities", juice, wipes, bandaids, etc.)* All right, Stephen, mommy has…left, she's, left and already she can't wait to see you for you to come back…. Stephen, come on now, any jacket is…you know what, you should bring the red one, with the baseballs…you better hurry up though cause Dante is already…he's playing, he's jumping and climbing, and laughing, he's already fascinated by the littlest things, a trail of ants climbing up the side of a tree, cracks in the earth a dinosaur might have fallen through, a crevice simply waiting for a little boy to peer down and discover a whole t-rex or…I know you wanna be the first cat on the merry go round, the first…Stephen, mommy can't wait to… we're both waiting, Stephen…come on son…please… but you're not, you're not coming, are you…? *(Beat. Stephen does not come. He is left staring down the hallway.)* No. No, Vette, you never ask for too much— *(To* LEON*)* Your room is all set. There's food in the kitchen. I got to go.

LEON: Listen if you trying to get out of here, put up some more of them fliers—

MARCUS: You should get some sleep.

LEON: We both been up all night. I was hoping by now—

MARCUS: We was all hoping for better than what we got. But that's life, right? Salt and sugar.

LEON: You wanna tell me what the detective had to say?

MARCUS: He said he was upstate. He said he can't stand driving at night but he got a tip and he got up from his bed and he made the drive. (*He moves quickly to the stand, packs the gun in his backpack.*)

LEON: What you need that for?

MARCUS: I'm waiting for Colombo give me the same news he's been giving me for the past two weeks. But not this time. Somebody wrote a new ending.

LEON: Marcus.

MARCUS: He said, "I'll be back at the station, early. Meet me there, a little after sunrise." And now the sun is coming up and I need to go.

LEON: What he say about your boy?

MARCUS: Maybe I should have called Vette, right? She said don't call unless something changes. I mean, the minute he said it, "I'm sorry, truly, but your son is dead," I didn't want to believe anything had changed. Right? Because this is my son, my child, he cannot be... But he is. Everything has changed.

LEON: Give me the bag, Marcus

(LEON *and* MARCUS *scuffle a moment for the bag.* MARCUS *comes away with it.* LEON *is simply tired.*)

MARCUS: Colombo! He said the man who killed my son is so simple he probably don't even know what he did! Can you believe that! A grown man, sucking his thumb, took him right to a shallow grave and when they broke the earth, everything was red. Red jacket red...Stephen has always been mahogany. Mahogany!

LEON: I'm sorry son, I should'a known something, felt something.

MARCUS: I don't even have to murder the whole world, just this one simple minded man.

LEON: Marcus, I ain't come here to let you do nothing like this.

MARCUS: I *know* you ain't come here for this. You came here for some peace of mind or closure or 'cause your sugar's bad or some shit for Leon Goodwater.

LEON: Let's just take a minute. Don't do this just 'cause you don't wanna be me.

MARCUS: Everything I do is not to be you! (*Pulls the .45 out of his backpack*) Sometimes, *this* is what love costs. What do you know 'bout that?

LEON: (*He stands square in the doorway.*) Nothing. But if I had to bet my life on it, I'd say you *got* to be here. You got to be here for what you love, for Stephen, for your wife. If you ever didn't wanna be me, Marcus, this is the moment.

MARCUS: (*He points the gun at* LEON.) I ain't ask you to come in here...like you got some kind of wisdom! You can't come in here in one night and be my father!

LEON: That's fine. I'm just gonna stand here.

MARCUS: My son is dead! You wanna do something for me? All I need from you right now is to move out of my way.

(LEON *simply shakes his head "no."*)

LEON: That's the one thing I cannot do.

(There is the sound of a key opening locks in the door. LEON *rushes to take the gun and backpack from* MARCUS, *puts it in the backpack and goes down to the window to catch the last bit of sunrise.* YVETTE *steps in, bundled up for the weather.)*

MARCUS: Yvette.

YVETTE: Marcus.

MARCUS: This is my wife, Yvette. This is my father.

YVETTE: Hello.

LEON: Morning.

YVETTE: I woke up this morning, looked outside and I swear, frogs and blood started pouring out the sky, Marcus. You said just cause that isn't possible, doesn't mean it won't happen, but together, together we would go toe to toe with God…right?

MARCUS: That's right.

YVETTE: When did he call?

MARCUS: Early this morning.

YVETTE: And Stephen? My baby?

MARCUS: Vette—

*(*YVETTE *holds her hand up to stop* MARCUS.*)*

YVETTE: You remember, that first night, there was nothing here, nothing but you and me and Stephen?

MARCUS: I remember.

*(*MARCUS *goes to* YVETTE *and she simply lays her head on . his chest. They maintain this tableau until the end of the play.* LEON *has turned to look back out at the city.* BENARD *enters and begins to play, up tempo, speaking his language. The trumpet runs until he runs out of breath.)*

LEON: It's a shame, the hell we go through sometimes just to find a little something decent.

BENARD: That day, couldn't find a damn cab nowhere on the street. I run from that little place we rented all the way to the station. When I got to the platform, you and yo' mama was about to get on the train and I...you don't remember this but you was sho'nuf handsome! Barely walking but you had on that white suit with the short pants I bought you for Easter. That's right, clean as the board of health cause I made sure you and Mugg had what you was supposed to have!

LEON: No. You didn't. Maybe you did the best you could. Maybe you didn't. But that's all right. Look. Sunrise. *(He holds up his hands.)* And I'm steady. Better than I been in a good while.

BENARD: I was a man of my time, did what every generation before me did! When Mugg get here—

LEON: Daddy, Mugg...ain't...coming. On this side of the grave, where the clock is ticking, this is where you got to do whatever you can to love decent, from one moment to the next. *(He points to* MARCUS *and* YVETTE.*)* Look at'em over there. *That's* what eternity looks like. Midst of all this chaos, and look what they got. Look at what they *made. (He goes to the window to look out over the city.)* That's beautiful, right? *(Points to the horn)* You make sure and take that horn with you.

BENARD: I'll be damn. *(He exits.)*

END OF PLAY

* 9 7 8 0 8 8 1 4 5 4 2 0 8 *